# Alter Egos

### Edited by Amy Acre and Jake Wild Hall

PRESS

**Alter Egos**

Published by Bad Betty Press in 2019
www.badbettypress.com

Cover artwork: 'i got a sick feeling / a knot in the pit of my stomach' by Bobby Parker

Printed and bound in the United Kingdom

A CIP record of this book is available from the British Library.

ISBN: 978-1-913268-02-2

Supported using public funding by the National Lottery through Arts Council England

Supported using public funding by
**ARTS COUNCIL
ENGLAND**
LOTTERY FUNDED

# Alter Egos

You are stronger than you believe. You have greater powers than you know.

– Antiope

We are what we pretend to be, so we must be careful about what we pretend to be.

– Kurt Vonnegut

Now we must outfilth the asshole or assholes that sent us this, and then they must die!

– Divine

# Contents

# Introduction

When Amy and I came up with the idea for this book, my immediate reaction was of ridiculous joy, for I believed I was about to fulfil a lifelong dream by publishing a book of Avengers fan fiction, and limericks describing the Marvel Cinematic Universe as the greatest franchise of all time.

As it turned out, we settled on a more varied and nuanced interpretation of 'alter egos', and I am overjoyed with the outcome. The poems we received are an exploration of ourselves and others in a truly honest way. And what better way is there to discover people than to ask what they want us to see in them? How honest you can be when you play with your own reality.

Sometimes an alter ego is a mask we wear to be stronger, to brave a world where we feel panelled in. Other times the alter ego is the true self, the one we are when we are safe and bold. But where does an alter ego come from? Is it a reflection of a memory we wanted to be, an aftershock of a relationship, a picture we draw?

Or is it as simple as Superman and Clark Kent—are they heroes? If that's the case, maybe all heroes are just as broken and fragile as any of us.

## JAKE WILD HALL

One thing I've taken away from these poems is that we create alter egos so that we can talk to ourselves, and to others. They're often drawn from real life heroes—parents, older siblings, film stars—and worn as a way of getting under their skin, or of touching someone otherwise out of reach.

Those real relationships can be fraught with a complex blend of adulation, envy, resentment and love. But if you can become your idol, absorbing the sublime, you can transfer this to a much simpler state of communion.

Through social media, we've all learned how to turn ourselves into superbrands, admired from afar for what we are not, or as hyper, more saturated versions of ourselves. Like regression therapy, putting on an alter ego allows us to retrace our steps and enact a kind of therapeutic process towards catharsis—whether by righting wrongs, reclaiming power or just being more honest about who we are. Placing your ego outside of yourself also makes it easier to self care, as it so often feels more important to be kind to others than to ourselves.

Sometimes it's the self we wear every day that is the mask, and some of the alter egos in this book are clearly those false selves—the ones we think others want us to be. Someone more typical, healthy, heteronormative, or happy than we really are. Or even someone we used to be, held onto still, but ultimately lost.

Alter egos can be invoked in times of pain or glory. They can also be a safe place to hide. In superhero stories, the alter ego is usually the hero's geekier, less formidable cousin. In real life, our alter egos are the ones who are bigger, louder, more glamorous, but their function remains the same. Like in the film *High Anxiety*, when Mel Brooks and Madeline Kahn get through airport security by pretending to be a loud and annoying elderly couple, noise can be a disappearing trick.

The poems in this book stunned me with their beauty, their humour, and the bubbling intensity of the relationships explored—between self and other, and between self and self. They call on gods, they play hide and seek. Shadows and ghosts, drag kings and queens, absent fathers, secret lovers, lone wolves. Maybe there's a little bit of Marvel in here after all.

AMY ACRE

# HEROES

# Alter Ego 1: Isabella Rossellini in *Death Becomes Her*

her mouth shape/ the word *cardamom*

skin tone/ scorpion milk

you could boil a diamond down to liquid
still she'd walk it

9 years old & drinking
her through the TV

a boy is not meant to *get* glamour but
this plunging neckline is life!

a flowing smoke-grey coat with clam shell collar
the vital points of lacquered nails/ tapping a bourbon glass
& how about that frosted planet of Fabergé egg

these are the women which men like me swallow

we live through their cool/ their sense of
ease with themselves
that is everything

*Everything*

I had no gun as a boy
no air rifle/ no pistol/ no plastic PK47

but let's say that I'd had

it would have been a revolver
something drawn from a clutch with a crisp snap to it

something that would look good in a fishnet-gloved hand

a silver dream/ in a web

MATTHEW
HAIGH

# Black Superman

After sex. I knocked on your chest hoping
there would be nobody inside who might
climb to my temple peak and offer peace.
Thought you would give me all of Superman,
love a body that forgets it can breathe,
pay ode to a homeland that lets you in.
It is not your job to save me from me,
but imagine my sorrow when I heard
a hero still inside your bones—quiet.
I want him, I want him to scale that black
that you buried in your mama's kitchen,
the day she explained to stop lingering.
That man was a legend before he learned
how to wear a suit, code-switch, make money and
grit. Your superpowers are far greater,
super strength lifted me and my burdens,
x-ray vision tore right through my armour,
there is more... I know because I heard him,
he asked to lay his qualms by my feet while
swaying back in that kitchen to music
his mama once played. I knocked on your chest,
hoped I could witness that power ascend.
I only met one man with that much strength.

# BIRDSPEED

# Pa

Does he like crumpet butter on his 'tache?
In the restaurant did the squib of my sad chatter come from upstairs, or down,
or the chairs, or the pasta, or the speakers, or near,
or far?

Does he find it easy as it looks?
When he jumps across the boulders does he feel like an ibex, or a goat,
or a bighorn, or a mouflon,
or a chamois?

Is the devil in his detail?
Does he keep his hearing aids in a case, or an intricate box,
or a small velvet bag with a drawstring,
or a jar?

Does he pretend he doesn't pray?
At Sainsbury's does he say much obliged, or 'preciate it,
or thank you, or thanks, or cheers,
or ta?

Why didn't he come to graduation?
Does he like his feats of nature deep, or erotic,
or bioluminescent, or quiet, or epic,
or bizarre?

Was he harried by a bully in after-school club?
Would the melody of his anthem be played on synth, or theremin,
or sound box under bald spot, or heartstrings, or tears,
or guitar?

Did he mean to teach his daughter the art of warfare?
Does he daydream I die gracelessly by Segway, or submarine,
or hot air balloon, or dinghy, or hovercraft, or crane,
or car?

Does he sniff his fingers after picking at his toenails?
How self-conscious does he feel when he enters a raffle, or a traffic jam,
or a lobby, or information, or a habit, or a country,
or a bar?

Was he glad when I was born?
Has he ever fucked off with a fire chief, or a philanderer,
or an Ofsted inspector, or a sylph, or a nightmare, or a gasman,
or a czar?

Does he know what some men are?
Has he ever had trouble with an engine, or a substance,
or a friend, or the law, or mental health,
or a bra?

Was it easy to keep me a secret from his family?
Does he know what I mean when I say gun, or cuss,
or rinse, or boy,
or par?

CAI DRAPER

# Where were you, Fassbender?

Who needs no other name.
When I'd outplayed all my characters
and outstayed all my welcomes
and remained a lonely imp in the corner
as it always had been.

Where were you, Rosamund Pike?
When the dream had stopped rowing its boat
gently or otherwise, and I was forced
to take the long route through the mire.
I thought, Rozzie, how much your father
would have disapproved.

Where were you, Tom Hardy?
When I was destitute and on the streets.
Just tattoos for friendly reminders I was human
in fact, and had a voice, and a story.
I want you to know that I broke into the car
not because I was low, but because I was high.

Where were you, Gwyneth Paltrow?
When I was forced to burn your book
for heating or pyromania (I forget which),
and found out my paltry inheritance
contained fewer digits than I'd expected.
I'll be speaking to someone about that.

Where were you, Benedict Cumberbatch?
When they brainwashed me and banished me
and I had to flee for Gibraltar,
Barbary macaques hiding the gin.

Where were you, Imogen Poots?
When they took me to court
for evading the bedroom tax, even though
I'd only just finished bricking up my windows.
Which wing were you in?

Where were you, Hugh Grant?
When she cried out once
and had me running for her love.
Gutter snow crimping under these suede loafers
(and they weren't cheap), I was on my knees, Hugh,
begging her to keep me.

Where were you, Gemma Arterton?
When Venice was sunk by the Chinese
to make way for the new Odeon.

Where were you, Jude Law?
When my hairline resembled an M on my forehead.
Everywhere billboards proclaimed the beauty in all men
and I felt like dying.

And where the fuck were you, Helena Bonham-Carter?
With your double-barrelled answer to everything.
When I'd lost my nerve and forgotten my lines.
Forgotten it was all for fun.

CAI
DRAPER

# Looking for Calamity

*Calamity was not brought up with protection from the evils of the world...*
*she was not immoral but unmoral, with her upbringing how could she be*
*anything but...she was a product of the wild and wooly west*
—Dora Du Fran (1868-1934)

We were both whores at fourteen but your face
was taking on a cow's arse by the time we met.
So I became a Madam and you became a man?

They're still making shows out you, girl,
much prettier tales than your own.
Some, kind of, mimic your cussing and drinking

but, mainly, you've become a whip-cracking blonde
with hands on hips and eyes shining
and I never knew you could sing.

You worked in a crib at Three Mile Hog Ranch -
twenty soldiers in a night, still in their boots
*Tougher 'n' hell and to hell with the consequence.*

You figured *If a girl wants to be a legend*
*she should just go ahead and be one.*
But the bottle took all six foot of you down.

So where is the real Martha Jane
gone, with the shit, from the streets of Deadwood,
gone with the dead eyes of laudanum?

Where is my illiterate black-eyed girl,
my prairie dove with a love of whiskey
who just did what poor girls did, back then?

SUE
JOHNS

# A tribute to death and the Jonas Brothers

The only important band to reform this year is Busted.
Sometimes I dream of Charlie from Busted's
caterpillar eyebrows crawling all over
my spider plant in a vain attempt to get it to die
like he wishes the Jonas Brothers would die
for upstaging the Busted reunion.

As a teenager I saw the Jonas Brothers
support Avril Lavigne with two of my ex-girlfriends.
My at-the-time actual girlfriend got jealous.
Also my mum was there.

The prettiest Jonas Brother doesn't sing,
mostly the one who looks like a goat does
and I wonder whether he wishes his prettier brother would die.

Avril Lavigne did die
and was replaced by a doppelganger
named Melissa, who thought it would be a good PR move
to marry Chad Kroeger from Nickelback.
I often wonder why she didn't marry me,

but I do not have a voice like expensive cars
driving up a gravel drive and was never
featured in a Spider-Man soundtrack.
I am no-one's hero.

Melissa, née Avril Lavigne, almost died in 2018
and now really loves God, as a side effect
of not dying, and maybe that increase in devotional energy
is what brought the Jonas Brothers back.


CHRISTOPHER
LANYON

# Alter Ego 2: Sandra Bullock in *The Net*

unkempt shirt/ the long cream limbs
the panoply of pizza boxes

meant to signal lovelessness
unloved/ unlovable

I love the lovelessness

where do I get my feral cat
my one bedroom apartment

sign me up
I'll put my sad tulips out with the trash

you can see through the candy-striped
lights of gender/ be
whatever hot mess of worm
the heart desires

be a hacker sucking ramen
be a loner
be god
mango suntan in the garden

sad loser/ sweet problem

MATTHEW HAIGH

# SPIES

# Blue Tint on the Brown Feather

Become more precious than a home.

She swims downstream from the water treatment ponds
so the residue of the day can iridesce over her.

    With nails still as precious as homes
    become more precious than a home.

She cuts her morning spliff with the fluff
from her hoover's dustbag. She French kisses the sun.

    Become the nails they burned down houses for
    with nails still as precious as homes.
    Become more precious than a home.

She takes in fog and doesn't choke. She lets out mist.
She absorbs the difference.

    When you've been alight for days
    become the nails they burned down houses for.
    With nails still as precious as homes
    become more precious than a home.

She platinums her fingernails, caught catalyst
wrist deep in traffic flows.

Become the remains of your resolve
when you've been alight for days.
Become the nails they burned down houses for
with nails still as precious as homes.
Become more precious than a home.

She dries bracken and sells it to city boys with shiny shoes.
She slips the profits to Anonymous.

With the light on it right
become the remains of your resolve.
When you've been alight for days
become the nails they burned down houses for.
With nails still as precious as homes
become more precious than a home.

She outwalks every car her ex sends to tail her.
She walks straight through hills when she has to.

Become the blue tint on the brown feather
with the light on it right.
Become the remains of your resolve
when you've been alight for days.
Become the nails they burned down houses for
with nails still as precious as homes.
Become more precious than a home.

She outwalks every car her ex sends to tail her.
She lets out mist. She absorbs the difference
so the residue of the day can iridesce over her.
She walks straight through hills when she has to.

# ANNA
# KAHN

# Note to a Reader

$\cup \in i$

union
is an element of
the imaginary unit

$U \cdot I \vdash E\,(x \mid y)$

U and I
conditional
expectation

$U \cdot I \Leftrightarrow \approx$

U and I
if and only if
approximately

$U \notin I \notin U \notin I$

U is not an element of I
is not an element of U
is not an element of I

$U \oplus I$

U and I
symmetric
difference

$\neg (U \cap I)$

U and I
do not
intersect

$U \cdot I \rightarrow | - |$

U and I
implies
distance

$| - | \; || \sim$

distance
is parallel to
indifference

$| - | > U \cdot I$

distance
is greater than
U and I

$$U \cdot I < \|$$

and U and I
are less than
parallel

$$\sim \, \gg U \gg I$$

indifference
is much greater than U
is much greater than I

$$U \cdot I \, \sigma \, \varnothing$$

U and I
standard deviation
empty set

$$\because (U \cdot I) > i$$

because U and I
are greater than
the imaginary unit

IRIS
COLOMB

# Gift

On Christmas Eve,
I get the first
off-peak train
to my parents.

Sit opposite
another yuppie
on a pilgrimage
for mince pies
and nostalgia.

As she Googles
the top ten tips for
the best brandy butter,
I slip my hand
in her bag for life.

Take out the top
present, pop it
in my rucksack.

Spend the rest of the trip
watching wetlands wash
into watercolour.

In my head, I hear
her lungs rattle

as she rustles
through the bag
a sixth time.

Picture her dad's
o-shaped lips:
"the real gift is
that you came."

Feel guilty pudding
sitting heavy in the pit
of her sofa-belly
all afternoon.

As we pull
into Barnham
I hoist my rucksack
on one shoulder,
brush past
paper close.

"Sorry."
"You're alright."

Alighting, I walk
to the platform bin,
drop the gift in.

Stare at the shrinking
yellow windows,
wonder if
she's watching.

# Notes from Mykonos Beach at 4am

On the other side of town, where graffiti and stray dogs rule,
a church sits on a cliff waiting for the purple ribbon horizon
to pull up a new day, refusing to acknowledge the men
gathered in the shadows under its nose. The gentle sea

laps as if it doesn't know what they are doing either,
salty waves falling against rock face. Bodies swallowed
by darkness. Silhouettes standing, knelt. Writhing in worship.

I wonder which of these midnight disciples
have mortgages, or families back at their hotels.
How many wives are lying in resort bedrooms

remembering the man who named each breast
on their honeymoon, dreaming
of a husband who can sleep at night.


TOBY
CAMPION

# Learning to Swallow

Maisie would serve us doubles
and charge for singles after college.
If her supervisor was in earshot, she'd ask for ID
and we'd hand over our Nando's loyalty cards.
Vodka lemonades and cherry VKs, each week

I felt less red about being the only boy in the group.
We took turns choosing three tracks for £1 on the jukebox
returning to the table, waiting for the look
on each other's faces when our songs dropped. TLC
and Craig David, singing along like we were in concert.

One week the football was on.
Two brickhouse-built men, with the tattooed fists
and chipped shoulders I knew too well
stood at the bar
and stared at me.

The girls didn't notice.
The table caught fire
and the glue holding up my forehead melted
my teeth fell out and buried me
and the girls didn't notice.

Next round I ordered a pint of beer.
Maisie laughed. I went red.
She pulled me a half of cider
which barked when I grabbed its neck.
I shouted at the screen to hide the noise.

I couldn't look them in the eye
when my songs came on; Johnny Cash
or something else my dad might have played.
The girls mocked the deep voices and mimed along.
I didn't have the words.

# TOBY
# CAMPION

# Wonder

I walked past a man today who was wearing blue trainers.

I wondered where he got the blue trainers from.

I wondered whether he tried on different coloured trainers before settling on the blue trainers.

I wondered how much he paid for the blue trainers.

I wondered whether he realised the blue trainers didn't go with the jeans he was wearing.

I wondered whether he thought he looked good.

I wondered whether he didn't care whether they went with his jeans or whether he looked good or not.

I wondered whether he only wore them to walk home from work.

I wondered whether his big black rucksack had some smarter shoes for him to change into when he got to where he was going.

I wondered where he was going.

I wondered whether he was meeting friends for dinner.

I wondered whether he had a girlfriend or boyfriend.

I wondered whether his girlfriend or boyfriend would meet him there.

I wondered whether his girlfriend or boyfriend would be late.

I wondered whether his girlfriend or boyfriend would panic they were late and rush out of work and cross the road without looking and get hit by a car.

I wondered how many times the man would try and call his girlfriend or boyfriend as they lay dead in the road.

I wondered how sad he'd feel after finding out the news.

I wondered how guilty he'd feel for sitting around laughing and drinking with friends as the love of his life bled from the head.

I wondered how much he'd cry at the funeral.
I wondered all of this until I got to my front door and wondered
  if I was OK.


# CARL
# BURKITT

# HOSTS

# Men an Tol

The Men an Tol, the white stone hole
they passed me through to change me back
to what I was – it sang a song to me

At first I thought I heard a host
of angels all around, an iron chant
of consonants, a thousand twangling instruments

And then the knocking began
At first it was a gentle tap, a jokebook joke –
who's there wasn't funny, though

The more insistent the knocking became
the more that I didn't know
It's a lost child, the one born rosy and bright

that grows pale as her bones grow long

*

A voice came through the intercom
it said 'ok – hold still again,
there's one more scan – and then all done, sweetie'

And then I left the white stone hole,
they sat me up, they changed my gown
but still my face was wan

*

The doctor held the scan up like
a darkened looking glass; you looked
at it, you looked at me, and then could not look back

*

The Men an Tol, the white stone hole
they passed me through to change me back
to what I was – it sang a song to me

JO
DAVIS

# Learning to Drive

*The self-defence of Julie Gianni, Vanilla Sky*

"I swallowed your cum. That means something."

in other words

I am a person of stomach.
I do not un-clutch myself for just anyone.
Your body made me promises that felt safe enough
to drive along. You are the one who broke the guardrail.

in other words

Do you know how difficult it is pretending
to enjoy drinking beer. The bitter depth
of being your *buddy* foaming the back
of my throat. I am bloated with you.
I eat breakfast and cannot un-think your hips,
and yet you force me to sit in the bar
with you and laugh, as stories of other women
ooze over your chin and ferment in your lap.
You squeeze my thigh under the table,
invite me to your room and expect me
to fold over into your crash test dummy.
And I do.

in other words

Yes, I did Cameron Diaz my car off the bridge
with you in the passenger seat,
yes, I made a love letter of your face
across the dashboard. But
you were the one who chose to get inside,
who fastened the seatbelt of his voice
into my ear and told me to let go.
You are the only man I have ever
closed my eyes behind the wheel for.
You are the one who left me
soaked into hotel towels, alone,
knowing full well that was not the deal
your body shook on.

in other words

Sorry about the disfiguration and everything
but all you ever gave me was face.
I am the one who died.

TOBY
CAMPION

I am being drained by this Babylon
slowly and clinically.

Pierced at precious pressure points
with holes jabbed into joints for ease
of stain removal.

We the prime cuts
preserved for appetising presentation.

And the process persists like Sisyphus.

Slow globs spill and grow around our hanging bodies.
Punctured and pickled.

I am being picked apart.

Drip times drip
over the time it takes
for a body
to stop considering itself
alive.

## Seeping

# THE REPEAT BEAT POET

# Glitter Fists

It's difficult to cough up glitter discreetly.
I need to pretend not to have swallowed

a baby dyke last night (or this morning;
I didn't look at my watch to know
what time I should pretend this didn't happen at.)

The baby dyke hollers from my stomach,
boots kicking up an acid storm.

She threatens to cut her way out
with her cheekbones - not if I don't release her
but if I don't let her come.

Given as how I'm digesting her where she sprawls,
her lack of desire to escape seems unhealthy.

If she comes while she's completely inside me
I'll break apart; this is an inescapable fact
of lesbianism; so she'll have to wait.

I cough into a tissue and crumple it and feel like
a 19th century heroine disguising her consumption.

The young professional I'm out for drinks with says
*your breath smells like cologne* when she kisses me.
I'm pretty sure she can hear the baby dyke.

Both of these women are going to have
to remain nameless because I'm running out

of names to attach to women in poems.
I can already tell that neither of these two
will be repeat characters. Skip forward three dates

and the young professional kicks off her sensible flats
and props my knee up on her breakfast bar.

She reaches up into me and reaches up further
into the baby dyke like she knows exactly
what she's looking for and her wrist

has to be cramping but she fists her other hand
in my hair and gets both of us off at once

and just as predicted I break apart
and leave her and the partially digested baby dyke
staring at each other over my sodden

and suddenly empty underwear in a storm
of lungfuls and lungfuls and lungfuls and lungfuls of glitter.


ANNA
KAHN

# My Identical Twin

is weeping for clean air
iced-teeth calving on
clamped champagne glass
& biting down on too-brittle candy
lest it's the last good thing ever.

It's just sugar
that's all, but she'll take it alright.
Like the line she took/
the line she read
before the swerve on the road
shattering chronology
a nothing-to-lose preface
committing her.

She'd tried books as gumshields
but still the enamel splintered.
If only she'd had a nervous breakdown,
something with room for recovery,
we need more nervous breakdowns
they say.

& if her lips crushed the windscreen
they chose it
not the other way round.

The autopsy revealed that she
was dead before contact
before she'd even got into the damn car.

*On opening the thoracic cavity*
*and cutting through the pleura*
*the lung tissues were macroscopically normal.*
*However, under the microscope the alveolar walls*
*were found to be shot full of planetary*
*elements of mercury,*
*tiny droplets suspended in a*
*wash of pity and water which shared*
*the composition of the Atlantic from*
*a sunlit swim last summer.*

*The diaphragm was found to be flaccid*
*and likely had been ineffectual in facilitating deep respiration*
*or laughter for some years prior to death,*
*like a slack trampoline worn out in childhood*
*now collecting leaves.*

*Detailed examination of the great arteries was unremarkable,*
*however dissection of the heart*
*surprisingly revealed that it was devoid of arterial blood*
*(the really red stuff of balloons and hibiscus)*
*it was so empty that you could hear*
*footsteps echoing from one chamber*
*to the next. It was like a closed*
*museum and on closer examination*
*was short circuiting and making*
*an old telephone ring.*

*On entry into the abdominal cavity*
*the spleen was the size of a beluga's*
*and filled with plastic stars and critiques.*
*Nothing could get through it, nothing.*

(The coroner became melancholic
just contemplating it.
He had started a series of drawings about it all.)

My twin always told me to
swallow pride & collect the
scraps of freedom on the floor.
*Aren't you tired of pretending?* she'd said.
I'd listened to her occasionally
because of rivalry & noise
but now that's all I think of
in the important moments
of these quickening days.

RUSHIKA
WICK

# The Visit

When I thought about visiting you,
coming to see you
after all this time,
I imagined
your imaginings of me
when you got my letter
saying I am arriving.
You saw me
in your mind's eye,
white dress,
long hair flowing,
high heels making me tall,
elegant,
desirable.

You prepared a feast,
chilled the wine,
and I arrived
in my sensible shoes.

KATE B
HALL

# SPIRIT
# ANIMALS

# Transition

It's March. We climb
the rocky spine
of Lägern mountain,
a stegosaur among the hills,
asleep between winter
and spring. If she woke
she could sweep
Baden into the Limmat
with a flick of her tail.
On the summit we kiss,
feeling the nape of her neck
shiver. We tiptoe
through snow down her flank.
Will she wake?
The winds rise, releasing
brand new flakes.


ANJA
KONIG

i

I don't want to write a poem
about love
because I want to see it
as something that isn't
self-possessed
as a body
that doesn't step neatly into
the hole carved out
on someone else's sleeve.

That doesn't dance precisely
gently
to the rhythm
of romantic chords and
accords
not quite said
out loud,
called romantic,

but instead places sentiment
on a stage
shapes it into a Walrus
and watches it
scream at windows it can't
jump out of.

ii

I don't want to write a poem
about love
because my best friend
took the Walrus' place;
pushed out too many
narcotics
from their circular spaces
and tried to jump through.

iii

I don't want to write a poem
about love
when love is the place
of Walruses,
displaced through this
language.

The multiple Walrus,
next to the multiples
of Walrus
all still staring at love and the
cuffs it's carved itself into,
taking communication away
from itself
and jumping out of windows.

# CAT CHONG

This will contain a certain
lack of polish
it will look like it was rubbed
by the Walrus
clumsy flippers
is it wise
should I say
show
tell
language is easier to feel
around with fingers than
flippers
easier to
stroke
strike
I don't usually possess the
desire to apply boot polish to
language
even if it should materialise
underfoot
paving language
pavement meaning
sidewalk interpretations
we polish bodies when
placing them six feet beneath
the surface
do I repeat this with words
when they don't mean more
funeral for constriction
funeral for no more
funeral for demarcation
but which ground do we
mean
the edge of the surface we
walk on
or the existential break that
barriers what is known and
what is

was
will be
something to do with
potential and the unknowable
I found the Walrus again
in the soft passages of time
feeling its way around the
carpeting
but that's another debate
which could end in crisis
though only a small one
if the personal can be
considered small
in the grand scheme of
things
wherever you go there you
are
I said it
the Walrus taking pride in a
confession when it's meant
for it
I've said those words
to no-one else
in saying so you are
implicated
I blurt out
you behold
the self labelled I
the self labelled you
without reflexive pronouns
the self labelled them
the self labelled hurt
                    breathless
                    blue lips
                    black inside
it's all
                    cliché

something else to feed
why aren't you eating
passing
stars
trees
sheep
dilapidated horses
beer bottles on brick walls
faces
going
coming
walking
running
to wherever
lectures
multiple things with a single
name
named
marks on land
people
places
beds
something else to be seen or
sink into
days and dreaming
as if brain functions over a
lifetime look like a hotel
room lobby in which valets
push thoughts around on
golden trolleys
that shine
that have been recently
polished
fuck
we're back to polish again

CAT CHONG

# MANIFESTATIONS

# Evolution

I have old bus tickets and a blue lighter in my pocket.
You look at me –
my face is an advert for loneliness
and I know that you will forget me when I say hello.

Your hands are weapons –
they make me feel breakable and alive.

The flames of the fire
fight – flicker – Plato's cave
(are shadows more beautiful?)
I am drunk.
You say to me –
        *What are you doing here?*
I wish I were not here.
I wish I were a photon in a far-flung galaxy
waiting for a black hole to engulf me so I can cease to exist –
like candy cigarettes
or the Bali tiger – though I guess that would still be here if it had a choice.

I am failing at evolution in ways that a tiger cannot comprehend.


# NICKI
# HEINEN

# Reincarnation on the Upper West Side

On the last day but one of the old year a friend tells me (in
Spring on Columbus, chopped salad, sweet potato chips)

that this is just one of many lives, that each of us has already lived hundreds, and
that's why she is feeling so tired. And, frankly, who would choose to do this again?

*I would*, I say. Maybe it's my first one but I would totally do this again,
including the flu I am just over, for this moment, with this friend, right here.

I would do it again for the triumph of riding the Express straight through
Columbus Circle while everyone else waits for the Local,

for that Dumpling place on Essex where you can have dinner for two bucks,
and it's not even bad, for the Flat White at Grumpy's, pretentious, delicious.

But it's not just food and public transport. It's also Three Lives,
which survived Barnes and Nobles and Amazon, too.

It's waking up at six after sleeping all night in the deep sea among lantern fish
and not even getting up once to pee,

or backing into the spoon of you at night, when you're not snoring that much.
If I have done that a thousand times, then

I want to do it another thousand. *No problem*, I say. Let me be
a drop on the hot plate any time.

Marcia takes a ketchupped chip, raises it in a kind of salute, and says, *I am sure it's not your first one, I can tell.*

The waiter comes for the credit card, he is milk and cream, and I swear I have seen him before.

ANJA
KONIG

# Easter Sunday

The lucky ones are gifted rebirth.
We get to leave our histories in other cities,
resurrect them once a year in Facebook memories
or a face in the crowd that looks like
the friend who died in a car crash,
a face in the crowd that looks like
someone we hurt.

We are clean in our new homes.
We are men without pasts.

I am not saying I'm Jesus Christ or anything
but maybe a lesser deity,
son of the god of small victories
or the god of small failures.
Son of the god of deleting old tweets.
Son of the god of eating a bag of clementines a day.

CHRISTOPHER
LANYON

# Self-Portrait as an Apple Tree

I'm so espalier
Don't fuck with me I've had years of training

What's behind that wall you might ask
Well don't

I think we're good here, I've got
Apples, just like a normal tree

I can take it. You can take it
I'm so espalier

I am
I am


NATALIE
SHAW

# Ambition

What does a baby think it is?
When babies look at adults do they think
*that's what I'll be?*
Or are they expecting to just be a baby forever?
Or do they look at something like, say, a chair and think
*I wonder when I'll look like that.*
Do babies have ambitions?
Adults do all sorts of things:
send emails, jump out of planes, eat three Pringles at a time.
I guess it wouldn't be too weird if a baby
looked at a chair and thought
*I'd love to provide comfort and support for others.*

CARL
BURKITT

# Dysfunction in All its Forms

*After Emily Hana*

The detachable shelves in my student room
are uncanny. When I first arrived,
I had to crack them back into place
like the bones of a broken spine.
They still tilt slightly to the left.

I wake up at 3pm on a Tuesday.
My days have been sliding back by the hours,
as if someone has weighted them
at one end with a dense anthology of 16th Century poetry.

A six-month-old birthday card covers the binding
with unconditional messages of approval.

Our washing machine is uncanny.
It sounds like a pull-back toy
from a Christmas cracker, chewing hours
in its plastic wheels, chattering steadily away into the dark.

If I'm supposed to be racing,
the mess of time outside my bedroom door
is less a display of vanishing red lights
and more the swinging face of a pocket-watch.

I don't remember hearing the cycle finish,
and happen upon a damp heap of clothes the next day.

The door of the bike shed is uncanny.
Facing the light in the yard is effort enough,
and every time it opens, I'm reminded
that the nails in the hinges have gone missing.
The sun has a malevolent look about it.

I hoist my bike onto its back wheel,
and wedge it between the shed's opposite corners.
I catch my knee on the handlebars, suppressing a cry,
and stumble back. The sun melts corkscrews through my eyes.

The door limps on its one hinge.
The bike will probably be stolen.

I call maintenance, and in three to five days
they let themselves in, and make some improvements.
They straighten my shelves.
They fix our washing machine.
They nail down the shed door.
When they are finished,
everything functions perfectly, and

I feel distinctly alone.

JONAH CORREN

# NEMESES

# Call Me Daddy or Don't Call Me At All

Call me daddy and imagine we are framed
halfway up the stairs as a family unit.
Picture us stood pastorally,
with our two children under us, smiling,
thinking about how good of a dad I am,
how good I am at being alive
and packing their school lunches, scruffing
their hair and saying *good luck today kiddo*.

Or call me that and imagine I am your dad
and that I actually know what I am doing,
think of me staying up late for you concerned
and chain-smoking in the garden, spitting
swear words into the ground hoping
you'll hear them and rush home to me.

Call me daddy and imagine that I am okay
and that I am not trying to reincarnate my own dad
in smart men, who I dream of holding
hands with my mum and scruffing my hair.

Call me daddy again and imagine that the cock
twitching to fill the space between me
and your thighs is unrelated to my own dad
as I try my best to do the same.

JOE
ANDREWS

# Midas

Excavators yawn
above the open pit.
I crave. I hack
through centuries of ice.
Wheels slice through rock,
undermining glaciers.
I load debris, deposit spoil,
weigh down the tongue.
Dead ice slides into the valley.
Tailings unravel
along the Kumtor river.
I take a bite of ice, another.
I eat through soil,
through gravel, silt.
Gold fills my mouth, stops
my eyes. I carve,
I want.

ANJA
KONIG

# Oh to be a murderess, tra la li, tra la lum

You ran into me bodysurfing. You were made of thunder and mirrors.
You marshalled me to safety, the shark alarms sympathetic to your
cause. You smelt faintly of salt and horror movies, lurking there
beside the lifeguard, who declared me unharmed. You knew everyone
on the beach. Your message transferred into me as if by gravity,
like ink from a punctuating cartridge. You said you had a spare
beachside apartment to rent (you owned the building) and a wife
at home you'd like me to meet. You lied. You stood blocking your
door, nagging for my number. You grew taller than your chandelier's
talons, rounder than your cellar's aged barrels. You forced a pen upon
me, *I only want your number*, a beautiful combination of physics and
chemistry and engineering. I began to write on your grocery list
which included garlic and nappies. Your hands were too soon filthy
with rape and seed to fend off the nib and knob and mouth and
thrust tube that prefaced your shroud. You were my uncles, the hand
over my primary mouth, you were the bastard at every barbecue in
history, the flasher in the church, the man in every dark. You were a
poem I wrote with a cheap hotel pen instead of re-enacting your sad
opera for the police. I liked the sounds of you both, your click, your
clack, your leak of Chartres-blue blood. Your fatal snap.

SUSAN
BRADLEY
SMITH

# Poachers

Did your father feel a lightness in his breast when I,
pray-he-is-never-son-in-law boy, left? They stared
at my bird of paradise chest, had to put the TV on mute
to be sure that we fucked like wood pigeons. At
night we would sneak down to the swift estuary, to pick the
plump oysters and peck salt off each other's bodies. A flame's
flickering light lit your parents' faces; I watched your mother wavering.
The froth and spittle on your father's lips drew the outline
of a man more preacher than English teacher. His fluttering
heart thrummed a prayer for escape and his veins popped blue like
the springtime forest floor. I watched your mother, trembling. A
bas-relief of father's rage now playing on her features, a bird's
call ringing in the hollow parts of her. The rest left translucent,
her hand on his shoulder as light as a broken wing.

CHRISTOPHER
LANYON

# The Entertainer

A comedian
Applause                          I will run her down
A seasoned sinner

You love action
You love the chaos of woman
You clap to encourage a strip show

I embalmed my memories
I used duct tape
You cheer me on
~~To score~~
Through layers
~~To win~~
My audience

You love to laugh
You love the chase
You love explosions

At the finale
A pile of tickets dumped near
A girl not laughing.

# BIRDSPEED

# Rooibos

Six years in
I'll offer you
rooibos tea
and you'll say
"don't you know me at all"
and I'll drink
the whole pot
down to dregs
and sad lemon
looking for
the answer

LAURIE
EAVES

# Acknowledgements

Thanks are due to Burning Eye Books, who first published the poems 'Notes from Mykonos Beach at 4am', 'Learning to Swallow' and 'Leaning to Drive' in Toby Campion's collection, *Through your blood*.

Thank you Bobby Parker, for the wonderful painting 'i got a sick feeling / a knot in the pit of my stomach', which is featured on the cover of this book.

Thank you Laurie Eaves for proofreading, and Dean Atta for the kind words. Thank you to the friends who encouraged their friends to submit poems.

Thank you Arts Council England for supporting this book, and James Trevelyan for the brilliant advice.

# About the Authors

**Joe Andrews** is a Nottingham-based poet and maths teacher. They have also worked as the University of Nottingham's Poetry Society's Events Coordinator and their work has previously been published online in *The Esthetic Apostle*.

A poet and cultural historian, **Susan Bradley Smith** lives at the beach in the most isolated city in the world, Perth, where she is Associate Professor of Creative Writing at Curtin University, and in Rome, where she is Professor of Poetry at John Cabot University. An advocate for maternal mental health, she also works as a bibliotherapist. Her latest verse novel is *The Postcult Heart*.

**Birdspeed** is a British-born, Barbadian-raised writer whose work often explores Caribbean culture and folklore, afrofuturism, black feminism, mental health (especially in black, working-class communities), and the lingering effects of colonialism on the black body. Birdspeed's performance poetry incorporates dance and martial arts. She is the 2019 UK Hammer and Tongue National Poetry Slam Champion. She is a graduate from Leeds University (BA) and Surrey University (MA). Her non-fictional writing specialises in cultural and critical theory. She is published in Empoword's *The Windrush Anthology* (July 2019). Birdspeed is Barbadian slang meaning 'to move real fast' and is the alter ego of Safiya Kamaria Kinshasa.

**Carl Burkitt** likes to tell tales. He tells long tales, short tales, silly tales, sad tales and he likes to tell them online, behind a mic, in books, in schools or on the sofa to his nieces and nephew.

**Toby Campion** is a UK Poetry Slam Champion and World Poetry Slam finalist. He has performed across the country and internationally and his work has been featured on national networks including BBC1, Channel 4, E4 and on the Arts Show with Jonathan Ross. His debut collection, *Through your blood*, was nominated for the Polari First Book Prize and his work was highly commended in the Forward Poetry Prizes 2019. An advocate for the power of poetry in the lives of young people, Toby is director of UniSlam and founder of the National Youth Poetry Showcase.

**Cat Chong** is a London-based poet currently studying on the Poetic Practice MA at Royal Holloway. She has been published in QUAD magazine, in a collaborative project titled *Although Almost Nothing Survives*, and had work displayed at Senate House Library. In 2019 she became one of the founding members of The CT Collective; a poetry collective run by students on the Poetic Practice course that curates poetry readings in London and has collaboratively authored two pamphlets that can be found in the National Poetry Library.

**Iris Colomb**'s practice explores different relationships between visual and spoken forms of text. She has given individual, collaborative and interactive performances in the UK, Austria, Romania, and France. Iris' pamphlet *I'm Shocked* came out with Bad Betty Press in 2018, her chapbook *just promise you won't write* was published by Gang Press in 2019. Her poems have also appeared in magazines such as *Para·text*, *Splinter*, *Datableed*, and *Poetry Wales*, as well as in a number of UK anthologies. Iris is the Co-Editor of HVTN Press, and a founding member of the interdisciplinary collective 'No Such Thing'.

Hailing from West Dorset, **Jonah Corren** is an undergraduate student studying English Literature at The University of Birmingham. He is a prominent member of Writers' Bloc, the university's creative writing society, and runs their monthly spoken word event 'Grizzly Pear.' In February 2019 Jonah competed in UniSlam with the Birmingham team, winning the competition, and going on to perform at Verve Poetry Festival. Jonah often writes about missing home, missing lectures, and missing almost half of every day. He hates concrete, early mornings and people who can't recycle, and loves fields, singing, and lengthy vegan menus. And poetry.

**Jo Davis** is a writer living in London. Her poetry has appeared in publications such as the *Mays Anthology* and *Halcyon Magazine* and she won the Disability in Poetry competition. Her epic poem, *The Patchwork Epic of Waltham Forest*, was commissioned by the local council and picked up by Waterstones. She was a judge and editor for the *Mays 10* and for *Poets at the Mill*. She has a PhD in Musicology from the University of Cambridge, where she won the William Berkeley Squire Prize and ran Darwin College Poetry Society. Her writers' group, Coppermill Poets, received local government funding for its community projects. Her creative writing programme, Lick the Pencil, won an UnLtd Award for its work with disabled and disadvantaged children. She also worked as a checker for *The Guardian*'s star crossword compiler, Araucaria (John Graham). She has performed at various poetry nights including Nicki Heinen's Words & Jazz.

**Cai Draper** is a poet and performer from South London. His work has been published by Poetical, Burning House, Salo Press and others.

**Laurie Eaves** is a poet from the village of Yapton, West Sussex. He's featured at spoken word nights including Boomerang Club, Forget What You Heard, Extra Second London, Mouthpiece and Norwich Live Lit Lounge. He became a Poetry Rivals finalist in 2016, works regularly with The Poetry Takeaway and has work published in the Spoken Word London *Anti-Hate Anthology*, *Small Word: Wide World* (Allographic Press) and *The London Spoken Word Anthology* (GUG Press). Laurie's first full-length collection, *Biceps*, is being released on Burning Eye Books in 2020. He's been described as 'organised' by three people this year.

**Matthew Haigh** is a poet from Cardiff. He has published work in journals including *The Rialto*, *Poetry London* and *Magma*, together with anthologies from both The Emma Press and Sidekick Books, and a pamphlet with Broken Sleep Books. His debut poetry collection, *Death Magazine*, was published with Salt in 2019.

**Kate B Hall** writes poetry, haiku, reviews and fiction. She is a long-term member of the British Haiku Society, of which she was President until the end of 2018, and a member of the Blue Side Poets. She has published two haiku collections *Running for nothing* in 2004 and *Irises* in 2015. Her work is regularly published in magazines, journals and anthologies, including *Show of Hands* a pamphlet by Blue Side Poets. Her first poetry collection *The Story Is* was published by Bad Betty Press (2018). Kate lives in West London with her life partner Liz.

**Nicki Heinen** studied English at Girton College, Cambridge University, where she won the Barbara Wrigley Prize for Poetry. Her work has been published in a variety of magazines and anthologies, including *Magma*, *Holdfast*, *Rising*, *Tentacular*, and *The Dizziness of Freedom*, and was shortlisted for the Pat Kavanagh Prize in 2012. She was Commended in the Winchester Poetry Prize 2018. She founded and hosts Words & Jazz, a spoken word and music night at the Vortex Jazz Café, London. Her pamphlet *Itch* was a London Review Bookshop Book of the Year and has been reviewed favourably in the *Manchester Review* and *Tears in the Fence* magazine. She lives in North London.

**Sue Johns** originates from Cornwall and now lives in South London. Her second collection *Hush* was published by Morgan's Eye Press in 2011. Her latest pamphlet *Rented* by Palewell Press in 2018.

**Anna Kahn** is the host of the Unfinished Edits podcast. She's a London Library Emerging Writer and a Barbican Young Poet. Her work has been published by *The London Magazine*, *The Rialto* and *The Rumpus*, amongst others. By day she does something inexplicable in tech.

**Anja Konig** grew up in the German language and now writes in English. Her first pamphlet *Advice for an Only Child* was shortlisted for the 2015 Michael Marks prize. Her first full collection *Animal Experiments* will be published in 2020 by Bad Betty Press.

**Christopher Lanyon** is a mathematician, PhD student and poet based in Nottingham. Originally from Cornwall, he is slowly making his way northwards and hopes to be freezing to death in the North Sea by 2025. His poems have been published in *Abridged*, *Oneiroi*, *Strix* and Yaffle Press's *Whirlagust*.

**The Repeat Beat Poet** is Peter deGraft-Johnson (PJ), a London-based Hip Hop poet, broadcaster, and emcee who fuses stream-of-consciousness writing and Hip Hop culture to capture and extend moments of time, thought, and feeling. He has performed across the UK and internationally, at The Royal Albert Hall, Battersea Arts Centre, Ronnie Scott's Jazz Club, festivals including the Edinburgh Fringe and Brainchild, and on many picket lines. PJ produces and hosts the spoken word events Boomerang and Pen-Ting, performs regularly with Hip Hop label Imaginary Millions, and is the creator of the Hip Hop/Spoken Word radio show The Repeat Beat Broadcast. PJ was nominated for the Jerwood Compton Poetry Fellowship in 2019.

**Natalie Shaw** has a kind husband and children of varying sizes. By day, she thinks about data a lot. By night, her poems can be found in various anthologies and journals, most recently *Butcher's Dog* and *Firth*. She was commended in the 2018 National Poetry Competition.

**Rushika Wick** is a doctor and writer currently studying at the Poetry School. She has an interest in exploring how social contracts and conditions become embodied. She has been published in magazines including *Ambit*, *Litro*, *DASH*, *Cold Lips* and *Rx Magazine* and forthcoming in *3:AM magazine*, *Flocklit* and *The Mechanics Institute Review 16*. Her work has been included in anthologies such as *Word-O-Mat 2* and the *New River Press Yearbook 2019*. She has performed in London and Amsterdam and co-hosts the Bad Slide Projector poetry salon.

# Other titles by Bad Betty Press

*Solomon's World*
Jake Wild Hall

*Unremember*
Joel Auterson

*In My Arms*
Setareh Ebrahimi

*The Story Is*
Kate B Hall

*The Dizziness Of Freedom*
Edited by Amy Acre
and Jake Wild Hall

*I'm Shocked*
Iris Colomb

*Ode to Laura Smith*
Aischa Daughtery

*The Pale Fox*
Katie Metcalfe

*TIGER*
Rebecca Tamás

*The Death of a Clown*
Tom Bland

*While I Yet Live*
Gboyega Odubanjo

*Raft*
Anne Gill

*She Too Is a Sailor*
Antonia Jade King

*Blank*
Jake Wild Hall

*And They Are Covered in Gold Light*
Amy Acre

Forthcoming:
*The Body You're In*
Phoebe Wagner

*No Weakeners*
Tim Wells

.

Lightning Source UK Ltd.
Milton Keynes UK
UKHW040822210819
348226UK00002B/40/P